Wellington Ar
Marble Arch and Six
Great War Memorials

Roger H Bowdler and Steven P Brindle

CONTENTS

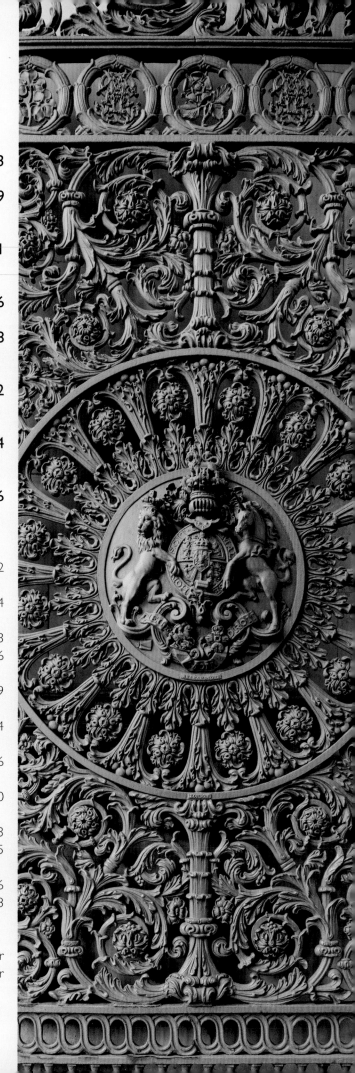

Wellington Arch

GEORGIAN LONDON

The great cities of medieval Europe were almost always surrounded by defensive walls and gates, and through the 18th and into the 19th centuries these city gates continued to be instruments of state and civic control, places where tolls and taxes were collected. In Britain, however, most city walls and gates were demolished in the later 17th and 18th centuries, reflecting the reduction in the power of the monarchy and of old-style city corporations. London's walls and gates were demolished piecemeal, and by the mid 18th century the rapidly expanding metropolis hardly seemed to have boundaries at all.

   As London grew and new suburbs spread outwards in all directions, it lost the character of a traditional European city. London's lack of grand gates was remarked upon, and many cultured Georgians felt that the city did not live up to its role as the capital of such a rich and powerful state. Several grand schemes for urban improvement were mooted. The Prince Regent (later George IV), with his architect John Nash (1752–1835), used the wealth and urban property of the Crown Estate to promote his grand designs for Regent Street and Regent's Park, and a number of other locations presented themselves as potential settings for grand architecture. The first, as one approached the city from the west, was Hyde Park Corner.

A WESTERN ENTRANCE FOR LONDON

Three large royal parks – Hyde Park, Green Park and St James's Park – set limits on the new suburbs of St James's and Mayfair, and in the late 18th century the idea had gradually formed that Hyde Park Corner, where the turnpike road from Kensington met Park Lane and Piccadilly, was effectively the new western entrance to London. This location was marked, however, not

Above: Engraving of about 1827 of the Quadrant and part of Regent Street, after a drawing by Thomas Hosmer Shepherd. Designed by John Nash, Regent Street was one of the first planned developments in London
Below: A watercolour of the entrance to Hyde Park, by an unknown artist, showing Hyde Park Corner as it appeared in about 1756

Facing page: Detail of the Wellington Arch gates, cast in iron at a cost of 1,700 guineas. The gates were restored to their original bronze-green colour between 2000 and 2001

Right: A design by Robert Adam of about 1775 for a triumphal gateway at Hyde Park Corner. His scheme was never realized

Below: This design by Sir John Soane for a grand entrance to London at Hyde Park Corner, with entrances to Hyde Park and Green Park flanking it on either side, was part of Soane's scheme for a monumental processional route to Westminster

by a grand gateway, but by a simple toll gate, where the Kensington Turnpike Trust collected money from road users. Designs for arches were made by the Italian architect Giacomo Leoni (1686–1746) in 1719, and the amateur Sir Thomas Robinson (1703–77) in 1761. Then between 1775 and 1778 the enterprising Scottish architect Robert Adam produced several alternative designs for a grand triumphal arch over the road flanked by entrances to Hyde Park to the north and Green Park to the south, but he was unable to interest the Government in financing his scheme. Instead, between 1791 and 1792, the Kensington Turnpike Trust built a new toll gate and lodges to designs by their architect John Groves Junior (1761–1811): the gates were of timber and absolutely plain, while the lodges were simple, elegant boxes, similar to those at the gates of many country houses.

A VICTORY MONUMENT

Britain's victory over Napoleonic France at the Battle of Waterloo in 1815, after 25 years of war, provided the impetus for a more ambitious approach to monumental architecture in London. Many now felt that London ought to have grand

buildings and victory monuments to rival those of Paris. Various architects produced further schemes for grand gateways doubling as victory monuments at Hyde Park Corner: Sir John Soane, one of the official architects of the Office of Works, developed two such schemes.

In the 1820s, however, the idea of a national victory monument became linked to George IV's (r.1820–30) great project to redevelop his parents' private residence, Buckingham House, into Buckingham Palace. The king did not like Soane's work, and he commissioned his favourite architect, John Nash, to carry out the palace scheme instead. Nash proposed to build a magnificent Roman triumphal arch, based on the Arch of Constantine in Rome, to commemorate Britain's victory

Above: The Hyde Park Corner toll gates in 1810. The plain brick house to the left is Apsley House, later transformed for the Duke of Wellington

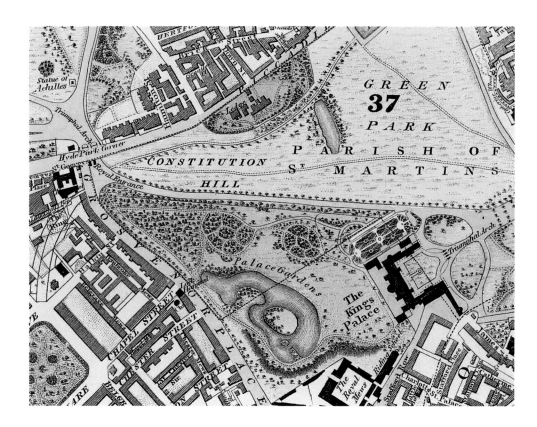

Above: Greenwood and Co.'s map of London of 1830 marks the original locations of the Marble Arch in front of Buckingham Palace, and the Green Park Arch opposite the Hyde Park Screen. The Green Park Arch is labelled 'Royal Entrance', illustrating its original intended purpose

Below: Portrait of Decimus Burton as a young man, shown in a lithograph of 1830–35, after a drawing by Eden Upton Eddis

over Napoleon Bonaparte (1769–1821) and act as the new entrance to Buckingham Palace's remodelled front courtyard; this developed into the Marble Arch (see page 20). Meanwhile, at Hyde Park Corner, the king and his advisors proposed that, instead of a grand city gate, a pair of magnificent entrances into Hyde Park and Green Park should be built, facing each other across Piccadilly. The Green Park entrance was to form an outer gate to the new Buckingham Palace.

DECIMUS BURTON AND THE GREEN PARK ARCH

In the summer of 1825, the Office of Woods and Forests instructed its architect, the 24-year-old Decimus Burton (1800–81), to design these two grand park entrances. Decimus was the tenth son (hence his name) of London's richest builder-developer, James Burton, and had been working on a project to landscape Hyde Park and build new railings and gates around it. For the new 'park entrances' Burton took his instructions from informal meetings of 'five or six noblemen' at Downing Street or Fife House. It was a very elevated group, which generally included the Prime Minister, Lord Liverpool; the Chancellor of the Exchequer, Lord Goderich; the Home Secretary, Robert Peel; Lord Farnborough, who was George IV's main artistic advisor; and Charles Arbuthnot, Secretary to the Office of Woods and Forests, which was paying for the scheme. In August 1825 Burton presented his first plans. The design for the Hyde Park Screen was personally approved by George IV,

who signed it with his initials 'GR'. It was built to this original design and still stands on its present site, forming a grand entry to the south-east corner of Hyde Park. Burton's southern Green Park entrance is the origin of the Wellington Arch.

Burton's initial design for the Green Park entrance, of 1825, was almost identical to the central part of his screen. It was designed to stand at the top of Constitution Hill, then a simple path through the park that led towards the front of Buckingham Palace. In September 1825, however, the Government decided that 'as the Archway was to form one of the Approaches to the Palace, it would be more respectful to His Majesty to have it upon a Scale and of a Character more ornamental than that of the Façade opposite'. In January 1826 Burton duly produced a second design for a more magnificent single-opening triumphal arch, with Corinthian columns rather than the simpler Ionic ones he had proposed for the screen. He made a model, now lost, and a perspective watercolour, showing the revised design, with the arch and screen covered in splendid ornament celebrating Britain's

Above: Decimus Burton's first design for the Green Park Arch, dated 1825, was rejected in favour of a grander approach
Below: Burton's watercolour of 1826 showing his revised design for the Green Park entrance – a magnificent triumphal arch with splendid decoration

Top: The Green Park Arch painted by James Pollard shortly after 1829. The Hyde Park Screen can be seen to the left

Above: *Burton's great gates, which were described by the* Morning Post *as being 'very fine – equal at least to any thing either in England or in any part of the Continent'*

victories over the French. It included carved trophies of weapons, figures of guardsmen 2.5m (8ft) high, a frieze of horsemen around the attic of the arch and a gilded-bronze quadriga, a four-horse chariot, on top.

THE BUILDING OF THE ARCH

Built of stock brick faced in Portland stone, Burton's arch was constructed to this revised design between 1826 and 1828. The arch's general form derives from ancient examples such as the Arch of Titus in Rome and the Arch of Trajan at Benevento, southern Italy, both of which have single openings flanked by engaged Corinthian columns (that is, partly merged into the body of the arch), but there is no close model for Burton's design. Burton also designed the magnificent gates, which were cast by the iron founder Joseph Bramah in his Pimlico foundry at a cost of 1,700 guineas. Between 1828 and 1829, with the arch nearing completion, Burton produced full-size drawings for its ornamental sculpture, estimated at an additional cost of £7,225. With the costs of the Buckingham Palace project soaring wildly, however (see page 22), the Treasury refused to sanction the cost of the sculpture. The scaffolding was taken down, leaving the arch incomplete.

Burton designed a simple landscaping scheme, and the arch lost its status as a formal outer entrance to Buckingham Palace, and was seen merely as a park entrance. It became generally known as the Green Park Arch. It housed rooms in a basement and three storeys on each side, which were apparently fitted out as a lodge-keeper's house and a police post (see page 12).

THE WELLINGTON MEMORIAL

After the victory at Waterloo in 1815, there had been a number of proposals for monuments in honour of Arthur Wellesley, 1st Duke of Wellington. A committee of 'Ladies of England' raised money and commissioned the giant nude statue of Achilles by Richard Westmacott (1775–1856), which was put up in 1822 close to Hyde Park Corner, and to Apsley House, the duke's London residence.

It was not until 1838, however, that a committee was formed to build a national memorial to the duke. The 62-strong Wellington Memorial Committee was dominated by a clique of three: the 5th Duke of Rutland, John Wilson Croker MP and Colonel Frederick Trench. A memorial in the vicinity of Apsley House seemed appropriate, and they resolved to place a giant equestrian statue of the duke on top of Burton's unfinished Green Park Arch. The trio forced their views through a poorly attended meeting of the committee, and had their protégé, the sculptor Matthew Cotes Wyatt (1777–1862), appointed to carry out the job. The Duke of Rutland then secured the Prime Minister, Lord Melbourne's, permission for the project. Other members of the Memorial Committee, feeling that they had been tricked and bypassed, reacted with fury, and when the designs became known they were vehemently criticized. Nevertheless, Wyatt was ordered to proceed, and it took him the next six years to complete the immense statue in a studio at Paddington. It cost £30,000, and stood 8.2m (27ft) high – so big that a person could have ridden on horseback beneath the bronze horse's belly.

Above: Richard Westmacott's statue of Achilles in Hyde Park, erected in 1822 to honour Arthur Wellesley, 1st Duke of Wellington

Below: Wyatt's model room as depicted in the Illustrated London News, 11 July 1846. The giant equestrian statue was made from 40 tonnes of bronze, most of it from captured French cannon

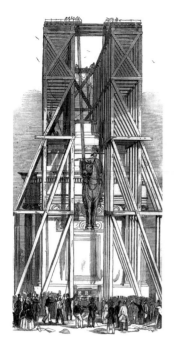

The statue was finished in 1845, and the Memorial Committee spent about £2,000 strengthening the arch to withstand its weight. Decimus Burton was asked to collaborate with Wyatt in adapting his arch to receive the huge and unexpected ornament. He was appalled by the scheme and complained about it bitterly, writing, 'it would be inappropriate to place a Colossal Equestrian Statue on a building which is small as a triumphal arch but huge as a pedestal'. The House of Commons condemned the design, and Sir Robert Peel's government became uneasy, offering the Memorial Committee other sites for the statue, such as Horse Guards Parade or Waterloo Place, but the Duke of Rutland refused to compromise. The statue and its proposed location were greeted with gales of hostile criticism, led by the satirical magazine *Punch*, which published numerous cartoons lampooning it.

The rows continued into 1846 when the Government withdrew its permission for the arch to be used, then reluctantly allowed the statue to be raised for a trial period. On 27 September 1846 the giant statue was taken on a special car pulled by 29 horses and accompanied by a grand military parade to Hyde Park Corner. When lifted into place it was greeted with such derision that the Government asked for it to

be taken down again, with the minister Lord Morpeth writing that the Government 'were not enabled to think the effect favourable to either the statue or the arch'. At that point, the Duke of Wellington himself finally ended the debate, privately indicating to the new Prime Minister, Lord John Russell, that if the statue were removed, he would feel obliged to resign all his public roles, which included Commander-in-Chief of the Army. Faced with this threat the Government backed down, and the statue remained in place despite the widespread view that it looked absurd. The Green Park Arch had been transformed into the Wellington Memorial, but the result was one of the greatest artistic fiascos of the 19th century.

THE ARCH IS MOVED

By 1874 Hyde Park Corner had become one of the worst traffic bottlenecks in London. From 1880 to 1882 a road-widening scheme, which involved moving the Wellington Arch, was planned. The Office of Works decided to rebuild the arch close to its original position, but facing down Constitution Hill. The arch would be set at an oblique angle to the Hyde Park Screen, breaking the original relationship

Above: The satirical magazine Punch *published several cartoons lampooning the Wellington Memorial in 1845 and 1846*
Left: Workmen posing by the statue of Wellington during its removal from the Arch in 1883

Facing page top: Drawing in the Illustrated London News, 3 October 1846, *showing the statue being raised onto the Arch. A team of riggers under the direction of a Mr McCullum, boatswain of Woolwich Dockyard, was employed to hoist the giant statue*
Facing page bottom: Photograph of the Wellington Arch with Wyatt's equestrian statue, taken between about 1870 and 1882

London's Smallest Police Station

For many years, the Wellington and Marble Arches were home to the Metropolitan Police.

The police had probably shared the Wellington Arch with its lodge-keeper from soon after its completion in about 1831, vacating it when the arch was moved in 1882. In April 1884 they moved back into the rebuilt arch. In the mid 19th century the management of large crowds in open spaces such as the royal parks was a matter of concern to the police, in the light of riots by Chartist activists seeking political reform. When the Marble Arch was rebuilt on its present site in 1851, the

Metropolitan Police's Chief Commissioner asked for it to be made available for the police patrolling Hyde Park. The rooms within the arch could accommodate a considerable number of officers in the event of a riot. The Wellington Arch, meanwhile, was

London's smallest independent police station, right up until its closure for the Hyde Park Corner improvement scheme in about 1959.

Below: Sergeant Cecil Pollard writing a report, with Snooks the cat looking on, Wellington Arch, 1952

Below: The Wellington Memorial now stands on a hill in the military town of Aldershot. It was relocated there in 1885 at the suggestion of the Prince of Wales (later Edward VII)

between the two monuments across Piccadilly. The contractor John Mowlem offered to dismantle and rebuild the arch for £24,291 in October 1882, and the work went ahead over the next two years. The rebuilt arch housed a park-keeper's lodge and a small police station.

The dismantling process revived the question of what to do with the giant statue of the Duke of Wellington. The Academicians of the Royal Academy united to sign a strongly worded petition, urging that this 'incongruity' should be removed, 'relieving this city from a blot which has long been a source of annoyance to Englishmen and of derision to foreigners'. The Office of Works considered melting the figure down, but many Army officers had contributed to the Wellington Memorial fund, and they objected. In 1885, the Government paid for the statue to be re-erected on a hill near the garrison church at Aldershot, the home of the Army, where it remains today. To replace it, the Government commissioned the sculptor Sir Joseph Boehm (1834–90) to make a more reasonably sized equestrian statue of the duke on a pedestal flanked by figures of guardsmen. This fine monument still stands opposite Apsley House.

ADRIAN JONES AND THE *QUADRIGA*

Decimus Burton died in 1881. He had loathed Wyatt's
Wellington statue, and left £2,000 to the Government towards
its removal from the arch. He died too soon to see his wish
realized when the arch was moved, but he would surely have
viewed the result with mixed feelings, for his arch still lacked
most of the sculptural decoration that he had designed for it.
Furthermore, his composition of arch and screen had been
broken. Shortly after his death, however, the arch became the
focus of another ambitious artistic project. In 1891 the sculptor
Adrian Jones (1845–1938) exhibited a plaster composition
entitled *Triumph* at the Royal Academy: a quadriga driven by a
boy charioteer and pulled by four wildly rearing horses, with
a winged angel descending upon it. The quadriga represented
the forces of chaos and war being calmed by the angel who
represented peace.

*Above: Late 19th-century postcard
of Hyde Park Corner with the
Wellington Arch in its new location.
Sir Joseph Boehm's statue of the
Duke of Wellington, erected in 1888,
can be seen to the left of the arch
Left: Adrian Jones's original plaster
sculpture* Triumph, *which he
exhibited at the Royal Academy
in 1891*

Adrian Jones: Leading Equestrian Artist

Jones's long experience as a vet gave him an outstanding grasp of animal anatomy and made him the leading animal sculptor of his generation in Britain.

Born in Shropshire in 1845, Adrian Jones was interested from an early age in painting and the natural world. His father pressurized him to join the Army, but Adrian proposed a compromise: he trained as a vet and entered the cavalry in that capacity. In 1867 he joined the Royal Horse Artillery at Ahmednagar in India and served as a veterinary captain for 23 years.

Throughout this period he produced sketches and paintings of dogs and horses, later turning his hand to

small-scale figure sculpture. Jones exhibited his first small bronze at the Royal Academy in 1884, and by the time he retired from the Army in 1890 he had developed a successful second career as an artist and sculptor, taking a studio in Chelsea.

Although he was manifestly talented, he never felt fully accepted by the artistic establishment, and experienced a number of snubs and slights. Despite this his career prospered, with significant commissions for the royal family including the life-sized sculpture of the Prince of Wales's horse Persimmon (1895), which still stands at the

Royal Stud, Sandringham. Other major public commissions for large-scale monuments included the Royal Marines Memorial in The Mall (1902), the 2nd Duke of Cambridge's statue on Whitehall (1907) and the Cavalry Memorial, now in Hyde Park (1924). The Wellington Arch *Quadriga* is his undoubted masterpiece.

Above: *Portrait by Alfred Priest, 1909, of Adrian Jones in front of his sculpture Triumph. Jones exhibited the work at the Royal Academy in 1891*
Left: *Adrian Jones's statue of Prince George, 2nd Duke of Cambridge, on Whitehall, unveiled in 1907*

The Prince of Wales, the future Edward VII (r.1901–10), is said to have admired Jones's composition, and suggested that a larger version of it would be an ideal adornment for the Wellington Arch. Jones was greatly enthused by the idea and produced a design for the arch crowned with a quadriga sculpture, although at that time there was no prospect of any money being found for it. Over the next decade Jones became one of Britain's leading monumental sculptors, his talents being demonstrated publicly in his equestrian statue of the 2nd Duke of Cambridge on Whitehall (1907).

Between 1907 and 1908 the architect Aston Webb (1849–1930) designed grand new gate-piers and gates for either side of the Wellington Arch. These were built as part of the Victoria Memorial Scheme, which involved landscaping The Mall and remodelling the area in front of Buckingham Palace as well as creating the Victoria Memorial itself. The Wellington Arch was drawn into this new ceremonial landscape, and assumed a meaningful visual role as an outer entrance to the palace area.

The Memorial Scheme probably helped to revive the idea of a quadriga, and in 1907 the Royal Household found a discreet donor – the banker Lord Michelham of Hellingly, a friend of Edward VII – who was willing to pay for it. Jones calculated that it would cost £15,615 to make the *Quadriga*, which included £6,000 for his own work for three years and £7,000 for casting it in bronze. This figure proved to be an underestimate and Jones ended up effectively subsidizing the work himself.

Below left: Jones and his assistants taking tea inside the plaster mould of one of the Quadriga *horses*

Below right: The structural framework for one of the horses, upon which Jones applied modelling clay

Bottom right: One of Jones's assistants working on the fine detail of the clay model for one of the horses

Below: Finally completed in the summer of 1911, the Quadriga *was assembled as a test at the AB Burton foundry, where this photograph of the statue and foundry workers was taken*

CREATING A MASTERPIECE

Jones made the giant composition in his studio in Chelsea: it was so big that he had to model one element at a time, and he could only judge the total effect when the whole sculpture was complete. Each horse began with a metal armature covered with timber framing, over which he applied modelling clay. When each figure was complete, Jones commissioned Italian specialists in plaster-casting to make a plaster mould around it; this was then cut away in sections. The pieces of the mould were then reassembled and used to make a full plaster cast.

Jones took three years to model the whole group; he was visited by Edward VII several times during the process. The plaster casts were sent to AB Burton and Company at Thames Ditton, one of the leading statuary foundries in Britain, which cast the giant figures in bronze from 1910 to 1911, each horse being made in seven pieces. The arch was given a new roof with steel girders to support the *Quadriga*, and the sculpture was erected in January 1912. Although there was no grand unveiling ceremony, the *Quadriga* remains Jones's greatest work.

WELLINGTON ARCH TODAY

Traffic at Hyde Park Corner became increasingly problematic, and from 1959 to 1962 the Hyde Park Corner roundabout was created, with a short underpass beneath it. The arch was effectively marooned on a large traffic island and its gate piers to either side were destroyed. The scheme had further consequences for the arch: the new underpass needed a giant shaft to vent smoke in the event of a fire, and the north side of the arch was adapted for this purpose. Its interiors were gutted, though this is not apparent from the outside.

The Wellington Arch then languished, neglected and empty, until its transfer to English Heritage in 1999. The arch and *Quadriga* were cleaned and repaired, the interiors were refurbished, the viewing galleries were created and it opened to the public in 2001. Since then, further highway alterations and landscaping have made Hyde Park Corner more accommodating for pedestrians and the island has become a destination for thousands of visitors, who come to appreciate the arch and the splendid group of memorials around it.

Above: Cleaning and repairing the Wellington Arch masonry during restoration work between 1999 and 2000
Below: The Wellington Arch and restored Quadriga from the north-west

Marble Arch

AN AMBITIOUS SCHEME

The Marble Arch is a well-known London landmark, giving its name to an underground station, a traffic junction and a district, but as with the Wellington Arch, its history is a saga of grand ambitions leading to disappointing, compromised outcomes.

When the Prince Regent succeeded to the throne as George IV in 1820, he began to make plans for a new palace in London. A number of different projects were mooted, but the king insisted that his new palace should be on the site of Buckingham House, the late 18th-century private residence of his parents, George III (r.1760–1820) and Queen Charlotte, as 'early associations' rendered it dear to him. He liked and trusted the architect John Nash, who had remodelled the fabulous Royal Pavilion at Brighton for him, and Nash began making preliminary plans to redevelop Buckingham House into the new palace. In 1825 Parliament passed a bill allowing the project to be funded from the Crown Estate. The king was an impatient client, however, and work had already started on site under Nash's direction. Nash's design retained some of the central block of the old house and its grand U-shaped entrance court facing east. From a very early stage, his scheme seems to have included a grand triumphal arch forming the main entrance to this courtyard from St James's Park.

The notion that such an arch should represent the nation's principal memorial to the great victory over Napoleonic France also seems to have formed part of the original concept. The idea may have come from Sir William Hillary MP, who in 1825 published a pamphlet in which he called for a victory monument to be built, and suggested that this could be a triumphal arch

'I am too old to build a palace but I must have a pied à terre … I tell him [Nash] I will have it at Buckingham House; and if he pulls it down he shall rebuild it in the same place; there are early associations which endear me to the spot.' George IV, as quoted by John Nash

Above: *Portrait of George IV by Sir David Wilkie, 1830*

Below: *Coloured aquatint of 1809 showing Buckingham House before Nash's redevelopment*

Facing page: *The south side of the Marble Arch*

sited 'to form the grand approach to the future royal residence of the British capital'. Inspiration may also have come from Paris. Napoleon Bonaparte had built the Arc de Triomphe du Carrousel, a magnificent structure based on the Arch of Constantine in Rome, as the ceremonial entrance to the Tuileries Palace between 1806 and 1808, and began the huge Arc de Triomphe at the western end of the Avenue des Champs Élysées in 1810 (it was not finished until 1836). These two Parisian arches might have given George IV and his advisors the idea of a triumphal arch outside Buckingham Palace, with the Green Park Arch (now the Wellington Arch) at the top of Constitution Hill as an outer palace entrance (see page 6).

NASH'S DESIGN

The arch was initially designed to be clad in Bath stone, like the rest of Buckingham Palace, but in 1826, the decision was made to use white Italian marble. Marble, with its glossy finish, high cost and association with imperial Rome, would enhance the arch's prestige and lustre. Nash was already planning to use the material on a large scale for the interior of the palace, and he engaged Joseph Browne, a specialist contractor, to source the stone. From 1825 to 1826 Browne was in Italy, buying large quantities of marble from the famous Carrara quarries in Tuscany. Fine statuary marble was chosen for the sculptures on the arch, with a slightly coarser variety known as *ravaccione* for the plainer areas. Numerous shipments were sent back to England between 1826 and 1829 for use in the palace and on the arch, to a total value of almost £25,000.

Like the Arc de Triomphe du Carrousel in Paris, Nash based his design quite closely on the 4th-century Arch of Constantine in Rome. As a result the 'Marble Arch', as it

Above: Portrait of John Nash by Sir Thomas Lawrence (1769–1830). Nash designed the Marble Arch to form a grand gateway into the entrance courtyard of the remodelled Buckingham Palace
Below: The Arc de Triomphe du Carrousel, which formed a gateway to the Tuileries Palace, Paris, and might have inspired George IV and his advisors to create a similar gate at Buckingham Palace

became known, and that in Paris look very similar. None of Nash's drawings for the arch survives, but a magnificent plaster model, probably made in 1826 and now in the Victoria and Albert Museum, reveals exactly what it was meant to look like. A wide central arch is flanked by lower side arches, separated by Corinthian columns, with a full cornice above. A high attic storey was meant to rise above the cornice, adorned with long relief sculptures. The east or outer side of the arch was intended to commemorate the Army and the Battle of Waterloo, while the west side, facing the palace, was to commemorate the Navy and the Battle of Trafalgar. Nash engaged John Flaxman (1755–1826), a leading neoclassical sculptor, to model the decorative elements.

THE SCHEME GOES AWRY

Work to build the arch did not begin until late in 1827, and this delay was to prove fateful. Nash gave the construction contract to Browne, who laid the foundations and built the brick core, as well as carrying out the fine marble work. The *ravaccione*

Top: This plaster model is now the only record of Nash's original plan for the design and decoration of the Marble Arch

Above: The south side of the Arch of Constantine, Rome, which inspired Nash's design for the Marble Arch

Above: Portrait of Edward Blore by
George Koberwein, 1868. Blore took
over the palace project after John
Nash's dismissal in 1830

Below: This satirical print of 1829,
after a drawing by William Heath,
shows John Nash at Buckingham
Palace, standing behind the Marble
Arch, being quizzed about the soaring
costs of the building project

marble was cut into large facing blocks and fixed to the
brickwork with iron clamps. The eight Corinthian columns were
cut from monoliths – single huge blocks of marble – with their
capitals copied from actual Roman examples. Browne built a
special hoisting machine to lift the big upper pieces into place.
By 1828 Parliament was becoming increasingly anxious over the
costs of the whole palace project. A Select Committee report,
however, vindicated Nash, and work on the arch continued.

John Flaxman had died in 1826, and in June 1828 Nash
engaged Richard Westmacott to carve the large reliefs, and
Edward Hodges Baily (1788–1867) and Charles Rossi
(1762–1839) to produce the sculptural figures and other
elements. The arch was to be crowned by a bronze equestrian
statue of George IV by Francis Chantrey (1781–1841).

By the summer of 1830 the arch had reached cornice level.
It was at this point, however, with costs soaring, that the whole
palace project fell into financial crisis. Nash and the palace
were assailed by vehement criticism from the media and
politicians. Soon after George IV died in June 1830 all work on
the palace and arch was stopped, and the project was taken
over by the Office of Works. Nash was sacked in October
that year, and his management of the project was investigated.
Large sums of money were owed to the furious Browne.

In 1831 a new architect, Edward Blore, was appointed to
complete the palace project as efficiently and cheaply as
possible. Blore recommended that the arch be completed
without Nash's intended attic stage, as 'the lower it is kept the
better it will look and the less will it interfere with the palace'.
Blore was planning to add an upper storey to the palace, and

Marble Arch Sculptures Relocated

Some of the magnificent sculptural decoration for the Marble Arch had already been made when work on the arch was suspended. It was reused in a variety of locations.

Edward Blore's decision to complete the arch without the attic storey robbed the building of its original purpose as a memorial to the Napoleonic wars. By that point, however, much of the sculpture for the arch had already been made. Blore was finishing Buckingham Palace at the time, and he used most of the long panel depicting the Battle of Waterloo and two of the three panels representing the Battle of Trafalgar, all by Richard Westmacott, to adorn the new upper storey of the palace.

They remain there today. Two more groups of relief sculpture had been made to go on the square plinth above the arch's attic: one representing Britannia with a lion and unicorn, by Edward Hodges Baily, and the other representing Europe and Asia (complete with camel), by Charles Rossi. They were used by the architect William Wilkins on his new National Gallery, where they can still be seen.

Further sections of relief sculpture made by Westmacott for the arch were not used at

the time and were sold. They were eventually discovered in a storeroom at Shepperton Studios in 1985, and were sold at auction. They include a relief of Nelson receiving the Spanish surrender after the Battle of Cape St Vincent (1797). Finally, Chantrey's great equestrian statue of George IV, which was meant to go on top of the arch, was eventually given 'temporary occupation' of one of the main plinths in Trafalgar Square in 1843: it has remained there to this day.

Top: Part of Westmacott's relief depicting the Battle of Waterloo, now on the courtyard façade of Buckingham Palace
***Above:** Chantrey's statue of George IV in Trafalgar Square*
***Left:** Relief of Nelson receiving the Spanish surrender, discovered at Shepperton Studios in 1985*

he wanted to decorate it with the relief sculptures Westmacott had made for the attic storey of the arch. The arch was completed to Blore's revised design in the second half of 1833, with Browne again acting as contractor despite the dispute over payment for his previous work. Browne was eventually paid arrears of £14,799 in October 1835.

The arch remained incomplete, without the majority of its commemorative sculpture and the magnificent bronze gates that Nash had designed. Samuel Parker, a smith and founder, had made most of the parts together with other decorative elements for the palace, but like many of the craftsmen he was not paid when the scheme was suspended and was forced into bankruptcy in 1832. In 1837 the gates were eventually assembled by the founders Bramah and Prestage. The 'VR' monogram was added to commemorate the accession of Queen Victoria (r.1837–1901) in that year.

THE ARCH RELOCATED

Top: Watercolour of the east front of Buckingham Palace from St James's Park, 1846, by Joseph Nash. His painting shows the Marble Arch in its original location in front of the palace
Above: *St George and the dragon in one of the Marble Arch gate roundels*

Buckingham Palace became the official royal residence of Queen Victoria after her accession to the throne in 1837, but soon became too small to accommodate her growing household. In 1845, she wrote to the Prime Minister, Sir Robert Peel (1788–1850), asking him to turn his attention 'to the urgent necessity of doing something to Buckingham Palace' owing to 'the total want of accommodation for our little family,

which is growing up fast'. Between 1846 and 1850, Blore was commissioned to add a new east wing to the palace, closing off Nash's U-shaped courtyard. The new façade was built absurdly close to the Marble Arch. In 1850 the Government decided to dismantle the arch and the contractor Thomas Cubitt (1788–1855) was paid to take it down. On 26 October 1850 *The Builder* reported that 'the marble arch has been taken down to the ground: every block has been numbered, and a drawing made of each course, with corresponding numbers on the blocks so that they may be exactly replaced hereafter'.

Below: Engraving of 1852 by E Walker showing Buckingham Palace after the completion of Blore's new east wing and the removal of the Marble Arch

A number of new sites for the arch were proposed, but Cumberland Gate, at the north-east corner of Hyde Park, was finally chosen. The arch was rebuilt by Thomas Cubitt in the spring of 1851, at a cost of about £3,000 and was finally completed on 29 March that year. Decimus Burton, designer of the Wellington Arch, created a new setting of gates and railings for the Marble Arch on its new site. In its new location, the original outer face looks towards Oxford Street. This side was originally intended as the military or 'Waterloo' side, with the naval or 'Trafalgar' side facing the park.

Decoration of the Arch

The relief sculptures that were incorporated onto the Marble Arch have only general allegorical meanings, such as the winged Victories in the arch spandrels and the laurel wreaths on the east and west façades.

The south façade of the arch has six figures of Victories in the spandrels by Edward Hodges Baily, who also carved the relief panels representing the female figure of Justice with a naval warrior **A**, and female figures of Peace and Plenty **B**. The carving on the north side is all by Richard Westmacott; female figures representing England, Scotland and Ireland, to the left **C**, and a figure of Peace with cherubs and trophies of war **D**, on the right.

Above: *Winged Victories on the south side of the arch*

Left: Postcard of about 1910 showing the Marble Arch following the road improvement scheme of 1908. Separated from Hyde Park, the arch was encircled by roads

Below: The north face of the Marble Arch as it appears today

Facing page top: Statue of renowned builder Thomas Cubitt, who rebuilt the Marble Arch in its current location in 1851

THE MARBLE ARCH TODAY

On its new site, the Marble Arch formed a grand entrance to Hyde Park. Since then, however, like the Wellington Arch to the south, the Marble Arch has fallen victim to highway engineering. In 1905 a Royal Commission discovered that Marble Arch was London's busiest road junction. In 1908 the London County Council moved the boundary of Hyde Park to the south, destroying Burton's gates and railings and isolating the arch on a tiny traffic island. Between 1961 and 1962 the Greater London Council made further changes, which accompanied the widening of Park Lane. These changes gave the arch a more generously proportioned island and provided more of a formal setting for it, though they could do little to overcome its overall sense of isolation. Cleaning works in 1994 and again in 2004, however, have revealed the beauty and quality of its marble facing, and despite its compromised design and setting it remains a striking architectural landmark.

Six Great War Memorials in London

Central London is the setting for some of the nation's most important war memorials erected in the aftermath of the First World War (1914–18). The six memorials explored here are those in the guardianship of English Heritage, and their fascinating stories reveal different approaches to the commemoration of the Great War.

The building of the Wellington and Marble Arches in the early 19th century, as well as other monuments, such as Nelson's Column in Trafalgar Square, reflected a nation's triumphalist desire to celebrate victory over Napoleon and to glorify its leaders and its capital city. From the late Georgian period onwards, however, London was also graced with increasing numbers of public statues that commemorated the nation's dead – those who had lost their lives serving Britain's Empire in conflicts far afield.

Although the Second Boer War (1899–1902) was a comparatively small-scale conflict, the nation's reponse revealed just how strong the commemorative urge had become. Volunteer soldiers had served alongside the regular Army, and in an era that placed greater emphasis on the citizen, no longer was it only the officers who were remembered on memorials erected across the country.

A Focus for Grief

This upsurge in the raising of commemorative sculptures peaked in response to the immense scale of loss in the First World War. The dead

seldom came home: where their bodies could be found, they were laid to rest near the battlefield. Mourners in Britain, bereft of individual graves, needed a focus for their grief. The response came at many levels: from the national memorial of the Cenotaph, through tributes to branches of the services, down to local monuments, sometimes devoted to individual business premises or streets.

Six Iconic Memorials

The six war memorials explored in this guide are united in reflecting the impact of the Great War, although they differ hugely in style and approach. They reveal different aspects of memorialization: the universality of death; the harrowing reality of combat; the vulnerability of human flesh; victorious leadership; the

sacrifice of the individual and the debt owed by civilians to the military.

Legacy of Commemoration

A hundred years later, the sacrifices of the First World War remain heartfelt. The remarkable public success of the *Blood Swept Lands and Seas of Red* installation at the Tower of London between July and November 2014 shows the enduring attachment that the capital still feels towards emotive tributes to the dead of the First World War.

Cleaned and conserved for another generation, in their different ways, the six Great War memorials described in this guide still speak of individual and collective losses and act as a focus for commemoration in a way that the grand arches and columns of the previous century do not.

Above: Detail of the figure of the shell-carrier on the eastern side of the Royal Artillery Memorial (see page 31)

Facing page: The Cenotaph (see page 38), adorned with wreaths on Armistice Day, 11 November, retains its power as a national monument, but still reflects individual grief, as it has done since it was erected in 1920

Royal Artillery Memorial

Unveiled in 1925, this outstanding memorial commemorates the 49,076 fatalities suffered by the Royal Artillery (the single largest unit in the British Army) in the First World War, along with almost 30,000 further losses in subsequent conflicts. Artillery played an increasingly central role in combat in the First World War, with over 70 per cent of casualties on the Western Front being caused by shellfire. Although generally positioned behind the front line, service for gunners was exceedingly hazardous owing to the effectiveness of enemy counter-battery fire. Service in the Royal Artillery was extremely arduous too, and the stylized figures and reliefs around the sides of the memorial powerfully convey the courage and endurance required for front-line service in the Royal Artillery.

THE COMMISSION

The Royal Artillery War Commemoration Fund established a sub-committee for the erection of a war memorial in May 1919, and secured a site on a traffic island at Hyde Park Corner from the Office of Works. Early in 1921 it turned to the sculptor and former infantry officer Charles Sargeant Jagger MC (1885–1934) for a design which specifically depicted the role of artillery in the Great War. This was produced in association with the architect Lionel Pearson (of the firm of Adams, Holden and Pearson) and a definitive design was presented in 1923. On the advice of Sir Edwin Lutyens and Sir Reginald Blomfield, the orientation was revised to point the gun southwards, rather than directly towards the Wellington Arch.

Above: Jagger working on the relief on the south-east corner of the monument. His depiction of the toil and horror of front-line action was unsentimental and unflinching

Bottom: 8-inch howitzers of the 39th Siege Battery, Royal Garrison Artillery, in action during the Battle of the Somme, August 1916

Facing page: The Royal Artillery Memorial from the south-east. The dominant 9.2-inch howitzer on the top of the monument is a vivid reminder of the role of firepower in the First World War

Above: Large crowds gathered to witness the unveiling of the Royal Artillery Memorial on 18 October 1925, covering the monument with wreaths and flowers

Below: Figure of the shell-carrier on the eastern side of the monument

Below right: The north-eastern frieze depicts a heavy battery of 60-pounder guns in action

It was finally unveiled on 18 October 1925 by HRH Prince Arthur, Duke of Connaught; such were the demands of finishing the commission that Jagger suspended work on all other projects for six months thereafter to recuperate.

A SCULPTURAL MASTERPIECE

Jagger's original conception consisted of 'a very simple idea, a big powerful howitzer on a base which would be characteristic of an emplacement'. Pearson designed a cruciform base on a several-stepped lower base, with stepped-back upper sections; the bronze statues are supported on projecting blocks. The four powerful bronze figures depict (from the north, clockwise)

a recumbent corpse, draped in an overcoat; a carrier, sporting shell panniers; an Artillery lieutenant, holding an overcoat; and a driver with outstretched arms, wearing a cape and heavy protective boots. Around the principal level of the base is a frieze depicting front-line active service, ranging from heavy guns in action to a relief of a horse-drawn 13-pounder battery under fire. On top of the base is a depiction of a 9.2-inch howitzer in Portland stone, one of the main heavy weapons of the Western Front. On both east and west sides of the projecting arm of the base an inscription remembers the dead of the 'Royal Regiment of Artillery' killed during the First World War, while around the upper level of the base run the names of countries in which the Royal Artillery served, some of which are repeated. On the north end a further inscription refers to the roll of honour buried below.

The combination of detailed depictions of the actuality of combat with stylized relief sculptures looked to ancient Assyrian sculpture and elsewhere for inspiration. The bronze figures, powerfully conceived, show Jagger's characteristic technique of modelling in built-up pieces of clay and leaving the surface finish unsmoothed and richly textured. The model for the officer was Jagger's comrade in the Worcestershire Regiment, Lieutenant Eugene Paul Bennett VC. The recumbent corpse is a very rare feature on British war memorials. Having encountered initial reservations, Jagger was insistent on the inclusion of a dead gunner among the figures, and even offered to pay for the casting of this figure himself. The inscription below the corpse, 'Here was a royal fellowship of death', is taken from Shakespeare's *Henry V* and was suggested by Jagger himself. To the south are additional inscription panels commemorating the 29,924 losses of the regiment in the Second World War, added in 1949.

Above: An Artillery lieutenant holding a great coat stands at the southern end of the monument

Charles Sargeant Jagger: Soldier and Sculptor

A decorated veteran of the First World War and one of the leading sculptors of his day, Jagger won an enduring reputation for his war memorials.

Jagger was born near Rotherham, the son of a colliery manager. He trained as a silver engraver in Sheffield and studied at the Royal College of Art from 1907 to 1911. In 1914 he won the coveted prize to study at the British School at Rome, but instead enlisted in the Artists' Rifles. Jagger saw extensive service as an infantry officer. Commissioned into the Worcestershire Regiment in 1915, he was wounded at Gallipoli and again on the Western Front in April 1918, when he won the Military Cross.

Jagger's work resonated with ex-servicemen, who admired his ability to depict front-line combat with vividness, while representing the humanity of the fighting soldier. Early in 1919 he began the large relief sculpture *No Man's Land* (now at Tate Britain), a haunting depiction of the macabre reality of static trench warfare. He made his name as a memorial sculptor with the heroic figures on the Hoylake and West Kirby Memorial, Lancashire (completed in 1922) and created powerfully modelled sculptures for several war memorials abroad, including the Anglo-Belgian Memorial in Brussels (1923). His memorial to the employees of the Great Western Railway at London's Paddington Station (also 1922) rivals the Royal Artillery Memorial as his finest work.

Top: Portrait of Charles Sargeant Jagger painted in 1917 by his brother, David Jagger

Left: Jagger's Great Western Railway Memorial, which stands on platform 1 of Paddington Station, remembers the 2,524 employees of the Great Western Railway killed in the First World War

LEGACY

The memorial's initial reception was mixed: Lord Curzon notoriously dismissed the memorial as 'a toad squatting, about to spit fire out of its mouth … nothing more hideous could ever be conceived'. It was well received by the regiment and by veterans at large, however, and it has steadily risen in critical esteem. Jagger was awarded the gold medal of the Royal Society of British Sculptors and elected an Associate of the Royal Academy shortly after its completion. It is now internationally recognized as one of the finest memorials to have been erected anywhere after the First World War. Its combination of sculptural force, boldness of conception, vivid narrative and humanity makes the memorial pre-eminent. Located close to the Wellington Arch and Apsley House, the memorial forms the largest single commemorative element in this prominent group of military monuments.

Above: The bronze figure of a dead gunner at the north end of the Royal Artillery Memorial is a unique feature on any major British monument
Below: *Hyde Park Corner from the north-west, in about 1930, showing the memorial on its traffic island*

Machine Gun Corps Memorial

The Machine Gun Corps memorial on Hyde Park Corner was unveiled in 1925. It was one of the last works of Francis Derwent Wood RA (1871–1926), a noted sculptor of his day, and is seen by many as one of the most perplexing of all British war memorials.

'THE SUICIDE CLUB'

The modern machine gun was invented by Sir Hiram Maxim in 1884 and by 1914 it was a standard weapon in the modern arsenal. In 1915 a separate unit, the Machine Gun Corps, was founded to improve the deployment of the weapon. 170,000 men served in its ranks. It was disbanded in 1922, so the memorial is a tribute to a lost unit as well as to the many thousands of fatalities which it had suffered. Known by some as 'the Suicide Club', this corps was not for the faint-hearted.

Above: Derwent Wood's figure of David holding Goliath's sword stands above the dedication to the 'glorious heroes of the Machine Gun Corps'

Right: Soldiers of the Machine Gun Corps operating a Vickers machine gun in an exposed position at Mouquet Farm, September 1916, during the Battle of the Somme

'Masks for Facial Disfigurement'

Francis Derwent Wood's war service in a London hospital may help to explain the unusual subject matter he chose for the Machine Gun Corps Memorial.

Above: An original prosthetic mask made for a disfigured soldier by Anna Coleman Ladd, an American sculptor inspired by Derwent Wood

Recent research has revealed the pathos inherent in the Machine Gun Corps Memorial: Derwent Wood understood better than perhaps any artist of his generation the impact of modern warfare on the human body.

Derwent Wood was well known as a leading figure in the 'New Sculpture', a movement which sought to reinvigorate the academic tradition through a rediscovery of sculpture's variety and its potency as a means of depicting beauty and emotions.

In April 1915, the respected Royal Academician became Private Wood in the Royal Army Medical Corps. He had answered the call from the

Machine-gunners were often in exposed positions and became targets for enemy attention.

The jarring biblical inscription – 'Saul hath slain his thousands/ but David his tens of thousands' – referred to the devastating killing power of its weaponry. Artillery may have been the main killer of the Great War, and gas the most infamous, but machine guns are forever linked with the slaughter of trench warfare and the ghastliness of frontal assaults by infantry, most notoriously at the start of the Battle of the Somme on 1 July 1916.

A PUZZLING DESIGN

The weapons depicted are Vickers machine guns, introduced in 1912, and which remained the standard British heavy machine gun into the Second World War. Each is garlanded with bay wreaths, an ancient symbol for victory. According to some sources, the depictions here were actual examples of machine guns, encased in bronze. This is unconfirmed.

Between the guns stands an exquisite nude male figure, inspired by Greek and Renaissance sculpture, representing David: he holds Goliath's giant sword and shows the vulnerability as well as the beauty of the human form. Once dismissed by critics as crass in its irrelevance to modern warfare, new scholarship has shed light on why Derwent Wood chose this specific iconography for the memorial (see feature below).

This memorial has had a chequered life. It originally stood on a small traffic island to the south of the Royal Artillery Memorial. Dismantled after 1945 because of roadworks, it went into storage and was eventually installed in its present position in 1962. A version of the figure of David was erected as a memorial in Cheyne Walk, Chelsea, but was stolen in the early 1970s.

Above: The rear of the memorial includes an inscription commemorating the 13,791 men killed and the 48,258 wounded, captured or missing of the Machine Gun Corps

commander of the 3rd London General Hospital, Wandsworth, who needed help tending to the gravely wounded men in his care. Wood's renowned skills as a modeller were soon put to work. Young men (and some women too), disfigured as a result of the wounds they had received on the front line, were prone to withdrawal and depression, fearful of their reception in civilian society. Wood set up a 'Masks for Facial Disfigurement Department' – known at the hospital as the 'Tin Noses Shop' – which created bespoke prosthetic masks, secured to the head by spectacle frames. Cast from the faces of the disfigured soldiers and painted *in situ* with extraordinary care to mimic the patient's skin tones, these innovative masks aimed to restore the lost features of 'mangled youth'.

By placing the physically idealized figure of David alongside the depictions of machine guns, Derwent Wood was expressing the valour of the Corps as well as alluding to the weapon's destructive impact on the human body.

Below: Derwent Wood painting a patient's new facial mask in situ

The Cenotaph

Below: The Cenotaph in Whitehall from the north-east. The flags on either side of the memorial represent the Royal Navy, the British Army, the Royal Air Force and the Merchant Navy

This Grade I listed monument in the heart of Whitehall is today the principal national memorial to the dead of Britain and the British Empire in the First World War and subsequent conflicts of the 20th century. It is the focal point of the annual national service of remembrance, held on Remembrance Sunday (the second Sunday in November), and versions of the design can be found in other cities around the world.

AN 'EMPTY TOMB'

The word cenotaph derives from the Greek for an 'empty tomb', and this structure was originally conceived as a focus for the commemoration of the soldiers of Britain and its empire who lost their lives in the First World War, and whose remains lie across the globe. Its designer, Sir Edwin Lutyens OM (1869–1944), was the foremost architect of his day and responsible for many of the outstanding commemorative structures raised by the Imperial War Graves Commission in the years following the First World War.

The present memorial is the second on this site. The original was a temporary structure, rapidly designed by Lutyens. It was made of wood and painted canvas for the London Peace Celebrations of 19 July 1919. Inspired by reports of an equivalent parade in Paris, with a catafalque to honour the dead of France, Prime Minister David Lloyd George requested that a similar structure be erected for this purpose in early July 1919. London's celebrations featured a triumphant march of victorious Allied troops; when they reached the memorial, they saluted the memory of their fallen comrades from Britain and its Dominions, over a million of whom had given their lives.

Above left: An early sketch design by Lutyens for the Cenotaph, dated 4 June 1919. A slightly adapted design was rapidly built in July 1919

Above: *Lutyens's temporary wooden Cenotaph was unveiled for the Peace Day parade, 19 July 1919. Originally intended to stand only for one week, it was finally removed in January 1920*

Bottom: *The permanent Cenotaph unveiled by King George V (r.1910–36) on Armistice Day, 11 November 1920*

A Symbol of Collective Grief

Designed as a monument to honour the absent dead of the First World War, the Cenotaph has come to be seen as the national shrine to the memory of the fallen from all recent conflicts.

Early in the First World War, the decision was taken to forbid the repatriation of the dead: they would remain where they fell, alongside their comrades, irrespective of rank or family wishes. Besides, in the explosive intensity of static warfare, almost half of all fatalities had simply vanished, with no known resting place. Millions of mourners in Britain were thus left with no graves to visit and no focus for their grief. War memorials across the land were erected in their tens of thousands, and plaques, scrolls and medals were issued to the bereaved by a grateful nation. A temporary shrine in Hyde Park, erected in August 1918, had started to attract much public attention, but what was lacking was an enduring place for the British people to share their sorrow and remember the sacrifices of their loved ones.

First unveiled in July 1919, Lutyens's Cenotaph soon attracted huge interest. Wreaths and flowers began to pile up and close to a million people made their pilgrimage to the temporary structure. 'You could scarce see the Cenotaph for the aura, the halo, the throbbing air that encompassed it,' commented the *Daily Mail*. 'Oh Mummy, what a lovely garden my Daddy's got,' one small boy was overheard to say, on seeing the floral tributes piled around the new permanent version in 1920.

Lutyens's austere and deeply dignified design rejected symbolism, bombast and specifics. The empty tomb may echo the resurrection of Christ, but its non-denominational form ensures its relevance to all of the dead of the Empire and to audiences ever since. Its message was one of the universality of grief and of the human cost of victory. The Cenotaph needed little adaption to include reference to the Second World War. Nearly a century on, it still stands at the very heart of national remembrance.

Top: *Members of the public laying floral tributes at the Cenotaph, November 1920*

Above: *Next of Kin Memorial Plaques, like this one, were sent to the families of men and women who died on active service in the First World War, to honour their individual sacrifice*

The public immediately took the Cenotaph to its heart, and what had started out as a temporary marker for a parade soon became a national shrine (see feature opposite). A permanent second version, in Portland stone, was erected by the Office of Works in time for the Armistice Day parade of 11 November 1920, which also witnessed the procession of the Unknown Warrior, on his final journey to burial at Westminster Abbey.

ICONIC DESIGN

Lutyens's design consists of a tall tapering pedestal. At the top is a closed tomb, surmounted with a large laurel wreath. On either end, at the upper corners of the shaft, are carved stone laurel wreaths suspended by carved fillets. The tall shaft of the pedestal employs entasis, a technique where the vertical lines are curved slightly outwards to counteract the optical illusion when looking up at the monument that it curves inwards. This effect was minutely calculated so that the vertical lines would, if continued, converge on a point 1000 ft in the air, while the horizontal lines are also fractionally curved and would share a radial point 900 ft below the pavement. Three flags, representing each of the armed services, are installed on each side of the base: Lutyens wanted these to be carved in stone, as on some of his other war memorials, but actual flags were used instead. Lutyens's earliest designs included a flaming urn, to be placed on top, but these were abandoned in favour of a simpler design. The finely executed masonry bears few inscriptions: the only one, beside the dates of the two world wars, reads 'The Glorious Dead', and was Prime Minister David Lloyd George's idea.

The Cenotaph's subtle classicism, devoid of imagery or religious symbolism, creates one of the most admired and copied memorials in the world.

Above: Photograph of Edwin Landseer Lutyens, who designed the Cenotaph, taken in about 1920
Below: *The Cenotaph, looking south towards the Palace of Westminster. The carved laurel wreaths were modelled by Francis Derwent Wood, who sculpted the Machine Gun Corps memorial at Hyde Park Corner (see page 36)*

Field Marshal Earl Haig Memorial

Field Marshal Earl Haig was Commander-in-Chief on the Western Front from 1915 to 1918. Still a controversial figure (see feature opposite), his undeniable importance as commander of the victorious British and Empire forces was honoured by Parliament with this bronze equestrian statue, placed close to the old War Office on Whitehall.

Prime Minister Stanley Baldwin suggested erecting a monument to Haig soon after the latter's unexpected death in early 1928. Haig, a former cavalry officer, may have died from injuries sustained while hunting. A limited competition for the work was won in 1929 by Alfred Hardiman RA (1891–1949), with a base designed by the architect S Rowland Pierce (1896–1966). Controversy soon arose, however, over the stylized character of the monument: Hardiman depicted Haig hatless, wearing an open greatcoat over his uniform and holding a scroll in his right hand. He is seated upon a powerful horse, its hind legs in parallel and its left foreleg raised; the horse's neck is arched, with its head drawn in on a short rein. Haig's widow had pronounced views on the depiction of her husband and sought a more naturalistic horse, but Hardiman's approach won through. The memorial was eventually unveiled by the Duke of Gloucester on 10 November 1937.

Above: Alfred Hardiman's bold statue of Earl Haig stands on Whitehall, facing the Cenotaph. The stylized classical horse, which embodies strength and forward movement, is restrained by the more naturalistic figure of Haig

Below: The completed statue being transported over Westminster Bridge to Whitehall in 1937

CONTROVERSIAL DESIGN

Hardiman came from a London family of silversmiths. He trained at the Royal College of Art, the Royal Academy and the British School at Rome, having won the 1920 Rome Scholarship. He was strongly influenced by classical sculpture, particularly that of a severe archaic character, and his work can also be seen on the exterior of London's County Hall. Winning the 1929 competition for Haig's statue was a major event in his career, but the complexities of agreeing on the design and in manufacturing the costly statue nearly ruined him.

Contemporary critics with traditional views took exception to aspects of the sculpture, such as the stylized horse, Haig's stiff posture and his bare-headed appearance. Although controversial in its day, it is now seen as a powerful example of inter-war classical statuary which strove to reconcile traditional modes of military commemoration with a contemporary idiom. Strongly rhythmic in outline, the mannered depiction of the horse contrasts with the closely observed portrait of Haig, and is among the last equestrian statues of military commanders to have been erected in Britain.

Above: Hardiman at work on the statue in his studio. His depiction of the horse proved particularly controversial: in a letter to The Times in September, 1929, Lord Mildmay of Flete described it as 'a horse which no real horseman would be paid to ride'

Haig: a Figure of Controversy

Haig remains a disputed military figure owing to the huge loss of life endured under his command during the First World War.

Douglas Haig (1861–1928) was the son of a wealthy Edinburgh whisky distiller. Commander of the First Army in 1914, he replaced Sir John French as overall commander in mid 1915. Haig was responsible for leading the British and Empire forces on the Western Front for three years of costly attritional warfare, including the Battles of the Somme, Arras and the Third Battle of Ypres (or Passchendaele) and his reputation remains disputed.

Haig's post-war standing was enhanced by his support for the welfare of ex-servicemen, particularly the wounded. He was created Earl Haig in 1919 and received a large award enabling him

to purchase the estate of Bemersyde in the Scottish Borders.

It was once common to belittle the senior commanders of the Great War as heartless and unimaginative tyrants, indifferent to high casualty rates and hell-bent on pursuing

a war of attrition, in which the weaker side would eventually collapse. Today, however, it is recognized that under Haig's leadership, the largest army ever commanded by a British general developed war-winning ways of fighting, including progressive deployment of tanks and aircraft, devastating artillery strikes and the skilful logistical support of a force of many millions of men. He retained the full confidence of the Army, although not of politicians, particularly Prime Minister David Lloyd George.

Above: Portrait of Field Marshal Earl Haig by Solomon J Solomon, 1919

Above: Victor Rousseau's bronze central group was cast by the AB Burton foundry at Thames Ditton, which also cast the Quadriga sculpture on the Wellington Arch (see page 16)

Below: The figure of Justice seated on the left-hand side of the monument. These high reliefs, made of Portland stone, are now very eroded

Belgian Gratitude Memorial

One of the most unusual war memorials in London, the Belgian Gratitude Memorial was unveiled in 1920 on the Embankment, directly opposite Cleopatra's Needle. It was a tribute to Great Britain from the people of Belgium, in recognition of the welcome extended to Belgian refugees fleeing the German invasion of Belgium in August 1914. This invasion led directly to Britain's entry into the First World War. Plans for a memorial arose in 1916 and the Belgian sculptor Victor Rousseau (1865–1954), himself a refugee in London, received the commission. Subscriptions were raised from Belgian troops, as well as donations from the Belgian royal family. Sir Reginald Blomfield RA (1856–1942) designed the architectural setting.

A POIGNANT ALLEGORY

The central group depicts a mother, drapery-clad and with a strikingly elongated neck, urging two garland-bearing children forward. According to the sculptor, 'I designed the group representing Belgium as a woman draped in mourning, in the act of telling her children that Belgians will never forget their debt of gratitude to Great Britain. The garlands and other floral offerings borne by the children are symbolic of the wealth of the nine Belgian provinces. As for the children themselves, the

Belgian Refugees in London

The German invasion of neutral Belgium in August 1914 drove a million civilians abroad.

Many fled to Holland and France, but around 250,000 came to Britain (in addition to many Belgian soldiers). There was initial alarm at their arrival, and some protests took place. Overall, however, a more benign response emerged. A charity, the War Refugees Committee, was quickly established, chaired by Lord Hugh Cecil; responsibility for settling the in-comers soon passed to the Local Government Board. Many were housed temporarily in Alexandra Palace in Hornsey before settling elsewhere, and 100,000 alone passed through the Earl's Court exhibition centre. The Prince of Wales headed a charity, the Belgian Relief Committee, and across the land over 2,500 local committees were set up to provide succour for the uprooted arrivals.

The rapid expansion of the armaments industry became an important source of employment for the refugees. Many were engaged at the Vickers factory in Dartford, Kent, while in St Margaret's, Twickenham, a munitions factory set up by Belgian entrepreneur Charles Pelabon became the hub for a community of no fewer than 6,000 Belgians. The sculptor Victor Rousseau, meanwhile, was given a studio at the Royal College of Art and was warmly welcomed into the Chelsea Arts Club.

Above: Tea for 600 Belgian refugee children at Earl's Court, 1915

lad and the little girl are designed to typify the spirit of youth and the confidence in the future, which is the most marked characteristic of the Belgian nation.'

On the left is a relief carving depicting Justice, shown holding the 1837 Treaty of London which guaranteed Belgian neutrality, and matched on the right with one of Honour, represented as St George – both are now seriously eroded. At the top of the inset panels are relief carvings of the coats of arms of the provinces of Belgium.

The memorial was unveiled by Princess Clementine of Belgium on 12 October 1920, the fifth anniversary of the execution of nurse Edith Cavell, in Brussels (see page 46). Léon Delacroix, the Belgian Premier, made a speech referring to the self-sacrifice of British troops serving in Belgium; a parallel memorial in Brussels, sculpted by Charles Sargeant Jagger, was unveiled in 1923. The London memorial reflects the impact of conflict on civilian populations, poignantly expressed through the fatherless family group. It is also a rare example in England of Continental public statuary of fine quality.

Below: Photograph of Victor Rousseau, who designed the Belgian Gratitude Memorial, taken in about 1900

Edith Cavell Memorial

Nurse Edith Cavell (1865–1915) is one of the most renowned women associated with the First World War. Her memorial stands outside the National Portrait Gallery, just north of Trafalgar Square. One of the very earliest memorials of the war, it was commissioned by the *Daily Telegraph* soon after her execution by the German Army in October 1915. It was unveiled in 1920 by Queen Alexandra. The renowned sculptor Sir George Frampton RA (1860–1928) was its designer, and he undertook the work for free. Edith's sister posed for the figure, which is a rather idealized representation of the executed nurse.

Norfolk-born Cavell was in charge of a training school for nurses in Brussels at the start of the war. A woman of high principle, she refused to leave when the Germans invaded, but soon became involved in an escape line for Allied soldiers and would-be recruits, who were smuggled into neutral Holland in order to reach Britain. Finally caught, she was found guilty under martial law and shot by a firing squad. Her execution was a gift to Allied propagandists and she soon came to be seen as a martyr (see below).

Edith Cavell and War Propaganda

The execution of Edith Cavell evoked widespread revulsion in Britain and Allied nations and was exploited as a powerful symbol of German brutality.

Strictly speaking, the German authorities were operating within their martial laws when they sentenced Cavell to be shot. But in that twilight age of chivalry, this execution was seen by many as an outrage. The very idea of putting a middle-aged nurse in front of a firing squad was, to most, unthinkable.

The rightness of the Allied cause needed all the support it could get if it was to enlist the hearts and minds of the people, and, following the execution, recruiting posters across the Empire started to depict the scene, as did many popular prints. George Bellows, the celebrated American artist, included the scene in a series of lithographs showing alleged German atrocities in Belgium. The US Ambassador to Belgium had tried especially hard to secure the sparing of Cavell's life, and there

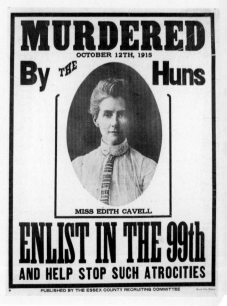

Far left: The lion on the north side of the monument crushes a snake beneath its paws and symbolizes Britain's victory over German spite and treachery

Left: The cross of the Geneva Convention, the symbol protecting humanitarian workers in fields of conflict, adorns the figure at the top of the monument and emphasizes Cavell's role as a nurse

'PATRIOTISM IS NOT ENOUGH'

The memorial, of marble against a granite setting, was unconventional in subject and design. At the top is a seated group with the larger figure, representing Humanity, sheltering an infant, representing the smaller states: it was for Belgium and Serbia that Britain had gone to war. The lion on the rear depicts British valour. The quotation of her final message, 'Patriotism is not enough. I must have no hatred or bitterness towards anyone', was only added later, when the National Council of Women lobbied to have a more forgiving, less martial, note to the memorial included.

Facing page: Looking north towards Sir George Frampton's memorial to Edith Cavell, shot at dawn, 12 October 1915

Far left: This poster, issued by the Essex County Recruiting Committee in 1915, uses the image of Edith Cavell to encourage men to enlist

Left: Commemorative medal by the French artist Victor Peter in memory of Edith Cavell, 1915. The nurse, looking resolute, is encircled by chains held by a sinister German officer wielding a revolver, a bat hovering over his shoulder

was widespread revulsion at her death in neutral America. The concept of 'Hunnish beastliness' became a staple theme in the propaganda war. Atrocities did undoubtedly take place, but few incidents were so forcibly portrayed as this one.

Streets and hospital wards were renamed after her; miniature china and brass figures were mass-produced; and after the war, other Cavell monuments were erected in Brussels, Paris, Melbourne, Toronto and Norwich, where her body was finally buried after a state funeral in Westminster Abbey.

Preserving the Memorials

The six London Great War memorials in the care of English Heritage have each stood for nearly 100 years. Safeguarding them for future generations is the work of expert conservators.

Located in the heart of London, surrounded by a relentless rush of commuters and exhaust fumes, collecting mouldering leaves mixed with the mess of city pigeons, and exposed to the extremes of weather, it is not surprising that these memorials suffer environmental damage. Periodic conservation is essential. Treatments include gentle steam cleaning and the removal of the detrimental mosses and algae as well as the repair of cracks on the carved surfaces to prevent the destructive ingress of water. The last steps are protective treatments – the tops of the monuments are given a breathable hydrophobic coating to resist the propagation of spores and carved friezes are brushed with a protective coating of lime and sands.

A Personal Perspective

Kimberly Reczek, a conservator with conservation firm DBR Limited reflects on her experience conserving the Royal Artillery Memorial at Hyde Park Corner:

'Like many, I have passed the Royal Artillery Memorial numerous times; and I have been aware of its large dark figures leaning against knobbled blocks as I cut across the loud traffic island. I knew about the significance of Jagger's creation, but it was not until I had the privilege of working on the monument as an arts conservator that I began to appreciate its power.

'Conserving the monument requires you to spend hours looking closely at the detail of the memorial. As the reliefs come into focus, you see a heart-breaking tangle of mud, machine, and limb; the howitzer sits where a noble steed traditionally would, and the bronze soldiers stare, haunted, into the distance. The bronze corpse laid out on the north side becomes all the more poignant when you notice the start of youthful stubble beneath the heavy wet hem of his coat. And every day, Royal Artillery mounted troops in groups of up to 50 soldiers saluted the monument as they marched past. My work on this memorial allowed me to witness this powerful connection between the living and dead.'

Above: Work to remove moss and algae from the Royal Artillery Memorial
Below: The Royal Artillery Memorial following conservation work